Hafiz in London. [Poems.]

Justin Maccarthy

Hafiz in London. [Poems.]
Maccarthy, Justin
British Library, Historical Print Editions
British Library
1886
viii. 90 p. ; 8°.
Ashley1090.

HAFIZ IN LONDON

PRINTED BY

SPOTTISWOODE AND CO., NEW-STREET SQUARE

LONDON

HAFIZ IN LONDON

BY

JUSTIN HUNTLY McCARTHY, M.P.

اگر بزلف دراز تو دست ما نرسد
گناه بخت پریشان و دست کوته ماست

London
CHATTO & WINDUS, PICCADILLY
1886

DEDICATION.

FERANGIS, at thy feet I lay

These roses from the haunted coast

Of Faristan, whose poets boast

Their Rocknabad and Mosellay ;

For I was in Shiraz to-day,

With ancient Hafiz for my host,

Who, like a comfortable ghost,

With Persian roses crowned my stay.

They are thy tribute from the land

Of Khayyam and our Khalifate,

For on their crimson folds of fate

A wizard ciphered with his wand

Words which I dare not here translate,

But you will read and understand.

CONTENTS.

HAFIZ IN LONDON.

HAFIZ IN LONDON.

HAFIZ in London ! even so.
For not alone by Rukni's flow
The ruddy Persian roses grow.

Not only 'neath the cypress groves,
With soul on fire the singer roves,
And tells the laughing stars his loves.

B

Here in this city—where I brood
Beside the river's darkling flood,
And feed the fever in my blood

With Eastern fancies quaintly traced
On yellow parchment, half effaced
In verses subtly interlaced—

Men eat and drink, men love and die,
Beneath this leaden London sky,
As eastward where the hoopoos fly,

And through the tranquil evening air
A muezzin from the turret stair
Summons all faithful souls to prayer.

And we who drink the Saki's wine

Believe its juice no less divine

Than filled, Hafiz, that cup of thine.

Master and most benign of shades,

Before thy gracious phantom fades

To Mosellay's enchanted glades,

Breathe on my lips, and o'er my brain

Some comfort for thy child, whose pain

Strives as you strove, but strives in vain.

When sundown sets the world on fire,

The music of the Master's lyre

Deadens the ache of keen desire.

Reading this painted Persian page,
Where, half a lover, half a sage,
You built your heart a golden cage,

My fancy, skimming southern seas,
Wanders at twilight where the breeze
Flutters the dark pomegranate trees.

We all are sultans in our dreams
Of gardens where the sunlight gleams
On fairer flowers and clearer streams ;

And thus in dreams I seek my home
Where dim Shiraz, dome after dome,
Smiles on the water's silver foam ;

The dancing girls, with tinkling feet
And many-coloured garments, beat
Their drums adown the twisted street ;

And while the revel sways along,
The scented, flower-crowned, laughing throng
Seem part and parcel of thy song.

Hafiz, night's rebel angels sweep
Across the sun ; I pledge you deep,
And smiling, sighing, sink to sleep.

MEMORY

SITTING silent in the twilight, faces of my former loves
Float about my fancy softly, like a silver flight of
   doves.

Brighter than the stars of heaven is the shining of
   their eyes,
Sweeter are their angel voices than the speech of
   Paradise.

I am old and grey and weary, winter in my blood and
 brain ;
But to-night these haunting phantoms conjure up my
 youth again.

Lovingly I name them over, all that world of gracious
 girls,
Almond-eyed and jasmine-bosomed, like a poet string-
 ing pearls.

In my tranquil cypress mazes just outside the sleepy
 town,
Blooms a tribe of laughing lilies fairer than a kingly
 crown.

Every lily in the garden wears a woman's gracious
    name,
Every lily in the garden set my spirit once aflame ;

And amongst that throng of lilies scarcely whiter than
    his hair,
Hafiz sits and dreams at sunset of the flowers no longer
    fair ;

Of the sweethearts dead and buried whom I worshipped
    long ago,
When this beard as grey as ashes was as sable as the
    sloe.

I would weep if I were wiser, but the idle child of
 song
Leaves reflection to the Mullah, sorrow to the Sufi
 throng.

Am I wrong to be contented in the sunlight to
 rehearse
Pleasant tales of love and lovers in my honey-laden
 verse ?

While the vinepress with the life-blood of the purple
 clusters drips,
I forget how slowly, surely, day by day to darkness
 slips,

Heedless how beyond the gateway in the field the
nations jar,
Hand on throat and hand on sabre in the trampled
lanes of war.

Ah! 'tis better on this pleasant river bank to lie
reclined,
While the ghosts of old affections fill the harem of my
mind.

Think no more of love and lasses, Hafiz; you can
scarcely hold
The Koran with trembling fingers. Hafiz, you are
growing old.

ELD.

HAFIZ, you are growing old ;

   Hafiz, all the girls abandon

Bards whose blood is getting cold,

   Bards whom Time has laid his hand on.

All the merry songs you sung

In the days when you were young,

Are not worth a feather's weight

To arrest the fist of Fate

   When it jogs your shifting sand on.

Hafiz, though a tinge of grey
   Shames the locks that once were sable,
Drink and laugh the world away,
   Swear that eld's a housewife's fable ;
Vow that youth is always yours
While the graceful gait allures,
While the perfume haunts the rose,
While a ruddy balsam flows
   From the flagon on the table.

Just a word within your ear,
   Hafiz : you're a craven creature
If you waste a single tear
   On the thought that every feature

Of the fairest face a maid

Ever showed the sun must fade ;

Rather bid your mistress weigh

Youth and beauty's barren stay,

    And a wiser lesson teach her.

Tell her youth was made for love ;

    Tell her wine was made for drinking ;

Tell her that in heaven above

    Mahmoud and his saints are winking

At the golden jest of youth ;

Tell her wisdom's wisest truth

Is, be merry while you may,

Cease regretting yesterday,

    Or about to-morrow thinking.

LONG AGO.

ALL my youth's desires are buried,
  Each within its narrow grave ;
Long ago their ghosts were ferried
  O'er Jaihun's enchanted wave ;
  Wild ambitions bright and brave,
  Loves that made me serve a slave,
All have slipped away like snow
  Long ago.

Stars in which my youth delighted
  Vanish from the heavenly band,
And I wander a benighted
  Stranger in a stranger land ;
  There is no one left to stand
  By my side or take my hand,
Of the friends I worshipped so
      Long ago.

One sweet name of all the number
  Haunts the chambers of my brain,
One sweet shape disturbs my slumber,
  Loved too well and loved in vain.
  Ah, Ferangis ! give again
  Half the pleasure, all the pain,

That my boyhood used to know

     Long ago.

These are dreams: I must remember

  That my youthful days are dead,

That the rigours of December

  Grizzle e'en a poet's head.

  Gone is gone, and dead is dead,

  And no roses bloom as red

As the roses used to blow

     Long ago.

Though my eyes pursue the swallow

  As he travels towards the sun,

Aged limbs refuse to follow

    Where the fancies lightly run.

    Hafiz, cease, the game is done,

    Life's fantastic robe is spun ;

Fate marked out the way to go

    Long ago.

You were passionate, my poet,

    In your manhood's golden dawn ;

Seized the seed of life to sow it

    On the tulip-tinted lawn ;

    Now you sit at home and yawn,

    Withered, grizzled, bent and drawn,

By the hearth : you scorned its glow

    Long ago.

What is left ? a sigh, a shudder,

For my past, and for the goal

Where, a boat without a rudder,

Drifts my tempest-troubled soul ;

Ah ! death's angel, taking toll,

Shall I find within thy bowl

Better wine than used to flow

Long ago ?

VANITY.

I DREAMT all night of your cold caresses ;
   Your kisses froze on my lips like flakes
   Of pitiless snow that chills and breaks
The warm heart snared in your sombre tresses.

I woke with a groan in the livid morning,
   Groaned and swore I would break away
   From the bitter bondage of love, and repay
Laughter with laughter, and scorn with scorning.

Ere noon was hot in the heavens, I met you ;

    You had but to smile as you passed, and lo !

    I was your lover again.   Heigho !

Hate you or love you, I can't forget you.

KAIF.

MINE be the musk and the music, mine be the laughing
girl ;
Mine be the ample flagon, brimmed with the blood
of the vine ;
Mine the divan encushioned, watching the dancers twirl ;
Mine the narghili serpent, breathing its soul divine.

Others can juggle with statecraft, others can lust for
command ;
Others can envy their fellows woman or vintage or
gold ;

Others can wrangle for title, fight for a rood of land ;

    Others think souls and bodies things to be bought

        and sold.

Such as they are, God made them ; such as they are,

        God guides ;

    Such as they are, they do their task, fill place in the

        world awhile ;

Such as they are, they eat and drink, and sleep on the

        breasts of their brides ;

    Such as they are, they sicken and die—may jackals

    their graves defile.

I for my part am happy, I for my part am calm,

    I for my part rejoice to the full in the hour that

        glideth by,

I for my part with all my heart delight in the vineyard's
balm,

I for my part will love and laugh till my moment
comes to die.

Grant me, Allah, digestion ; grant me, Allah, desire ;

Grant me a mistress with almond eyes and cinnamon-
scented breath ;

Grant me a golden vessel filled with the vineyard's fire ;

Grant me, Allah, a lazy life, and later a lazy death.

Dearest, I once was foolish ; dearest, I once was
young ;

Dearest, I once would have sold my soul for the price
of a passionate kiss ;

Dearest, you know what your lover was when the songs

of his youth were sung ;

Dearest, the devil deserves your soul for driving me

down to this.

YOU AND I.

SPARE your censures, worthy friend, on my love of
    drinking ;
Shut your senses, if you please, to the glasses clinking.

Only, while you rest with me, prithee keep your curses
For some other fellow's wine, other fellow's verses.

By what frenzy of reproof is your wisdom bitten ?
Are the sins that I commit in your volume written ?

If I run a tavern score, you don't pay the reckoning ;
If the Lotus-maiden nods, not to you she's beckoning.

Who shall say behind the Veil which is good and evil ?
Who shall say if you or I journey to the devil ?

Very varied laws of life you and I are firm on ;
Which of us, my friend, is text ? which of us is sermon ?

Every sober man or drunk seeks his soul's ideal ;
In the tavern and the mosque love alike is real.

Paradise is fair indeed ; but this side of heaven
There is joy in noonday sun, joy in shades of even.

Be not boastful of thy worth, for who knows when
    mounted
To the final judgment-seat how his sum is counted?

Sanctimonious folk like you, filled with moral phrases,
May be sent, to your surprise, packing off to blazes;

While poor rogues like us, who drink ere the vintage
    fail us,
May be plucked to Paradise from this very alehouse.

CONSOLATION.

WEEP not for the lost Yusuf, in Canaan his eyes shall
   close ;
Weep not for your wasted garden, it shall blossom like
   the rose.

Weep not for your nights of revel, weep not for your
   days of tears,
For an hour's repentance cancels all the sins of sixty
   years.

Weep not, soul with sorrow laden, once again the spring
 returns ;
Singer of the night, your planet once again in heaven
 burns.

Weep not for your boyhood's passions, weep not for
 your youth's despair ;
Every poet's heart was tangled sometime in a woman's
 hair.

Weep not, watcher for to-morrow, that thou never canst
 prevail
With the stars to tell the secret shrouded up behind the
 Veil.

Weep not if life's gloomy pathway terrifies your wandering soul,

For the byeway, not the highway, best conducteth to the goal.

Weep not for the loss of brother, grieve not at the gain of foe ;

Would you with Allah be angry when the winds of winter blow ?

Weep not, Hafiz, poor and lonely, but not all unhappy man,

While your life's as true and upright as ordained by Alkoran.

LOTUS.

I LOVE the Lotus-blossom when it wreathes
   Its painted petals in my sweetheart's tresses,
And she, enchanted by its odour, breathes
   Soft words of love, and soothes with soft caresses.

I love the Lotus-blossom when it lies
   On the white bosom of a sleeping woman,
And falls and rises as the dreamer sighs,
   For that love's sake she yet has told to no man.

I love the Lotus-blossom, for it grows

    On a lone grave beside a silent river ;

There my youth's mistress takes her last repose

    I loved, I hated, and I now forgive her.

PHILOSOPHY FOR OTHERS.

SALUTE the summer, breathe the breath of God,
   Be happy while you can, for by-and-by
   You that are now so full of life must die,
And redder roses blossom from your sod.

Believe me, brother, that behind the Veil
   A harp is touched, and one is singing to it
   A song of counsel, if you only knew it;
When wilt thou list, and let that song prevail?

D

Ask not poor Hafiz to admonish you
   With whom you should frequent, with whom
      drinking,
   For surely half an hour of tranquil thinking
Will teach you better what you ought to do.

The road that leads us to the Friend at last
   Is hard to travel, full of fear, temptation ;
   But think, my brother, think of the elation
In looking back along the road you've past.

Cease this perplexing problem to revolve ;
   Him the world clutches with a thousand finger
   Who on the pathway of his purpose lingers
To solve the riddle none were meant to solve.

For every flower that in the meadow blows,

    Is like a book.God opened to confess on

    His secret purpose.   But canst read the lesson

Writ in the purple petals of the rose?

And yet, O Hafiz! thou that talkest so wise

    Of prudence, and of patience, and compassion,

    Thy heart is all on fire with foolish passion

For one fair face and two tormenting eyes.

WISDOM.

WEEP not for the waning rose

Sigh not when the south wind blows,

Drown reflection in the can,

Dissipated Mussulman ;

Better to be glad than sad,

By the waves of Rocknabad.

If the truth must be confest,

Youth's a juggle, love's a jest,

Life's a comic caravan,

Discontented Mussulman ;

Better to be glad than sad,

By the waves of Rocknabad.

Eat your crust and drink your wine,

Deem the girl you love divine,

Make you merry for a span,

Philosophic Mussulman ;

Better to be glad than sad,

By the waves of Rocknabad.

RENUNCIATION.

THUS Allah makes proclamation :
    Ye that seek for peace of mind,
    What ye seek will only find
In the word renunciation.

Must I spill the wine I'm drinking,
    Must I practise what I preach,
    Ere Mohammed's hand will reach
Out to save my soul from sinking?

Must I shrink from soft caresses,
   Must I turn my eyes away,
   Must my heart no longer stay
In the tangle of your tresses?

Talk no more; I'll not believe it;
   Love is far too sweet to lose,
   And while wine is in the cruse,
By my beard I'll never leave it.

Hafiz, if the dedication
   Of thy being must belong
   Thus to woman, wine, and song,
Cease to preach renunciation.

AFTER RHAMAZAN.

THANK Allah ! the fast is over ;
  Thank Allah ! the feast is here ;
And at last each jolly lover
Of the vintage lives in clover
  Through the sweetest of the year.

Hide thy visage, sour ascetic ;
  Go thy ways, thy hour has past ;
While all revellers poetic
Join in union sympathetic,
  Drinking full and drinking fast.

Why should I incur reproaches
   If I like a stoup of wine?
Thank Allah! the hour approaches
When the jolly tapster broaches
   Liquor more than half divine.

He that drains a decent flagon
   At the wine house, can ignore
How the tongues of envy wag on.
Think how dull their days must drag on,
   Who run up no wine-house score.

For Allah's illumination,
   Shining on this rosy tide,

Finds no smug dissimulation,
Calling out for reprobation,
    Fair without and foul inside.

Clean our lives, our language civil,
    Alkoran's law understood ;
And we never let the devil
Catch us calling good things evil,
    And the things of evil good.

Where's the harm of my carouses
    With the vineyard's sanguine flood ?
If I drink till dawn arouses
All the Muftis from their houses,
    Do I drink my brother's blood ?

Hafiz, cease thy soul to trouble
  With the wherefore and the how;
Laugh and love, for life's a bubble;
Drink till everything grows double,
  And the roses leave your brow.

LONELY.

I AM lonely, very lonely, for the girl who stole my
    heart

Shines a star in other heavens, plays another lover's
    part,

While I sit in sombre silence, hearing how my heart
    will beat,

When I catch the faintest footfall sounding down my
    dreary street.

Is it she, or else some message sent from her to soothe
    my pain,

Falling on the thirsty seeds of passion like a holy rain?

No, the sounds die out in silence, and the twilight
deepens down,

And the orisons of evening breathe above the darkening
town ;

But my mosque is not the Mufti's, for my beacon in the
gloom

Is the crimson lamp-light floating from the tavern's
warmest room.

There I sit and drug my sorrow to a sleep that seems
like death,

There forget that I have ever kissed her lips and felt
her breath

From the parted smiling petals of the rose-flower of her
mouth

Breathe upon my eyes and hair the perfumes of the
odorous south.

It is war 'twixt wine and memory; on the tavern's
  trampled sill
I will plant my colours proudly, ruddy as the drops
  that fill
Yonder jars, whose prisoned magic slays regret and
  saps desire,
Burning folly from my bosom with the vineyard's liquid
  fire.
Woe is me! I boast untimely; even as I lift the cup,
On the purple flood the face of the beloved comes
  floating up.

COURAGE.

My soul rose out of its sleep, and said

There were angels once, but they all are dead ;

And heaven is empty, and cold and grey

As a world whose heat has burnt away.

The leaves of the tree of life are shed,

The bird who sang in the boughs has fled,

The coffin of night shrouds the corpse of the day,

And winter withers the mirth of May.

Allah and Shitan have gone to bed,

The prophets and saints are lapped in lead,

The shrines are shattered and no men pray,

The law is broken and none obey.

The roses of youth are no longer red,

Bitter life's wine is, bitter its bread,

The lips of the poets are stopped with clay,

And beauty fades into dull decay.

Then I turned me to Alkoran and read,

And Mohammed whispered, ' Hold up thy head.

Sin is an enemy hard to slay ;

Cry Allah 'l 'Akbar, and fight your way.'

VINE-VISIONS.

WHILE the House of Hope is builded on the weak and
    shifting sand,
While our breath is as the wind is, take the flagon in
    your hand ;

For while I was quaffing, laughing in the tavern yester-
    night,
From the unknown world an angel floated on my
    swimming sight—

E

Handed me a golden vessel, bade me drink, and as I
  drank
All my swooning senses straightway in the pool of
  slumber sank ;

And I dreamed a dream enchanted of a land beyond
  the sky,
Where no youthful cheek grows paler, where no flagon
  e'er runs dry,

Where no woman whispers falsely, where no eyes are
  ever wet,
Where no kisses ever weary, where no loving hearts
  forget.

Then I woke, and wept at waking, leaving in that
    pleasant land
Fairer flowers than Mosellay has, bluer domes than
    Samarcand.

Nevermore, unhappy Hafiz, will you tread that pleasant
    land,
Though you sucked the Seven Oceans from their cup of
    golden sand.

A DREAM.

I DREAMT, about the morning hours,
That in a field of scented flowers,
      By Rocknabad's cool flow,
      I saw Ferangis go
Swift by me like a dream of spring ;
And I, whose heart was hot to fling
      Myself before my dear,
      Stood full of silent fear.

And then I dreamt she came to lay
Softly her hand in mine and say,
    ' Hafiz, you yet shall know
      How happy is your woe ;
For what gift can the silent years
Offer so precious as these tears,
    And memory of the ache
      Your heart had for my sake ? '

Then, seeming stirred by pitying thought
Of all the joy I vainly sought,
    You gave your hand to kiss,
    Saying, ' Remember this

When you and I are grey and old,

When all this fiery love is cold,

  And, honouring lost delight,

  Keep your soul's whiteness white.'

I had no power to speak or move ;

Slowly the image of my love

  Faded before my eyes

  Like light from summer skies.

I wake and find Ferangis gone,

Yet scarce believe I am alone ;

  One minute since my hand

  Had touched her where I stand.

I read of men whom love made mad

In antique legends, softly sad

    As wind is after rain.

    I weep for Saadi's pain,

And stir the dust that lies above

Long shelves of poets crossed in love,

    To gain from their disgrace

    Some comfort for my case.

I find fit voices for my grief

In many a buried poet's leaf ;

    But, ah ! what ancient song

    Contains a charm so strong

That it shall make your heart confess
You love me, neither more or less ?
    Which learning, surely I
    Might be content to die.

And yet, when I reflect how fair
Those almond eyes and sable hair
    And gracious body are,
    I cry, ' Out of my star
Such beauty is ; ' I am as one
Who dreams of kingdoms till the sun
    Warns, if he would be fed,
    To rise and beg his bread.

Soft voices whisper in my ears,

'What girl deserves the grace of tears?

    Courage! the world is wide;

    Life's best is to be tried.

If this love fail, fresh loves await;

The reddest roses blossom late.

    Have you not passed before

    Out of love's curtained door?'

ATTAR OF LOVE.

THERE is neither pledge nor pity in the beauty of the
   rose
For the nightingale, whose sorrow in melodious madness
   flows ;

Though the brown bird sang for ever till its singing
   spirit fled,
Still the rose would greet the west wind with its petals'
   perfect red.

Once a songster in the garden chanted to a scornful rose,

'Cease thy scorn, for in the hedges many a fairer blossom
grows.'

Then the rose made answer smiling, 'Singer, thou hast
spoken sooth,

But no lover e'er addresses lover with so little ruth.

'Think not how the roses wither, be but gay while roses
bloom,

For the world's delight is little in the shadow of the tomb.'

Hafiz, if you sang more sweetly than the wind among
the reeds,

She you love is but the rose tree, and the rose tree never
heeds.

VAULTING AMBITION.

ONCE in my way an Arab story came
    Relating how a poet, drugged with wine,
    Watched from the tavern door where the divine
Pale moon lit all the sky with silver flame;
And crying, ' By Allah's eternal name,
    I swear that argent splendour shall be mine!'
    Leaped, clutching at the sky, and rolled supine
A muddy rascal, steeped in mire and shame.

This is our common madness.   Am not I

   Moon-haunted by thy beauty ?   Yet I stand

No farther from the empress of the sky

   Than from one touch of thy all-conquering hand ;

And though my songs made all the heavens sigh,

   I know you will not pity, nor understand.

A NIGHT-PIECE.

ONCE at night I paced my garden, seeking—but I
   sought in vain—
From the perfume of the roses balsam for my burning
   brain ;

For through all that dusk the circle of a single damask
   bloom
Shone more brightly than the cresset on a true believer's
   tomb ;

And so haughty in the splendour of her beauty burned
this rose,

That she banished from the bosom of the nightingale
repose,

While the eyes of sad narcissus floated o'er with loving
tears,

And the tulip bared her bosom wounded by a thousand spears.

Vainly then the lily offered to console the poet's care,

Vainly too the violet pleaded, 'Are no other blossoms
fair?'

Since the only potent rival of the rose tree is the vine,

Let me drown my hopeless passion in the Seven Seas of
wine.

' Hafiz, I conjure thee, from the rose tree pluck thy heart
away.'

Lo, the message is delivered, and the bearer speeds
away.

FALLEN ANGELS.

'TIS written in the Writing how a pair

Of angels dwelt with children of the dust,

And judged between the just and the unjust;

    Loyal to God, until a woman, fair

    As sun or stars, entangled in her hair

The hearts of those twin angels, and dark lust

Consumed them, till they whispered, ' Surely must

    We temper justice to a thing so rare.'

God punished those false angels, yet if I

    Were placed like them upon some judgment-seat

F

Speaking the law, and you came wandering by,

One smile of yours would fling me at your feet

Crying, 'Have pity upon me, O most sweet!

Do with me as you will, and let me die.'

PRAISE OF WINE.

ONCE again the ruddy vintage storms the chambers of
    my brain,
Steals my senses with its kisses, steals and yet shall steal
    again ;

But I do not blame the grape's blood for the vengeances
    it wreaks
When it plants its purple standard on the stronghold of
    my cheeks.

May Allah confer his blessing on the hands that pluck
the grape,
May their footsteps never fail who tread its clusters out
of shape.

Since the love of wine was written by Fate's finger on
my brow,
What is written once is written, and you cannot change
it now ;

Talk no babble about wisdom : in the awful hour of
death,
Is the breath of Aristotle better than the beggar's
breath ?

Spare me, pious friend, reproaches, for the selfsame God who chose

You to be so wise and pious, made me love the wine and rose.

Hafiz, spend thy life so wisely that when thou at last art dead,

'Dead' may not be all the comment, all the requiem that's said.

HAROUN ER-RASHEED'S POET.

KHALIFAH HAROUN, surnamed Er-Rasheed,
  In the calm evening of a festal day,
  Ordered his bard, Abu-l'Atahiyeh,
To praise the life it pleased his lord to lead.

The poet bowed and stirred the silver wires,
  And sang, ' Khalifah, peace and pleasure wait
  Within the shadow of your palace gate,
And deep fulfilment of your heart's desires.'

Said Haroun, smiling, 'Here is silver speech
    That shall be sealed with silver; speak again,
    And find my bounty boundless as the main
Which knows, so poets say, no further beach.'

Again the poet's voice and lute allied,
    'Let not the day star nor the night star shine
    Upon the hour that leaves a wish of thine,
Thy lightest wish, Haroun, ungratified.'

Still Haroun smiled, 'This time thy words are gold,
    And shall be guerdoned with a golden fee;
    Sing on, sweet voice, sing on and comfort me,
Nor ever fear to find thy master cold.'

Then sang Abu-l'Atahiyeh aloud,
　'In those dark moments when thy faltering breath
　Shall strive in vain against all-conquering death,
These things shall seem like shadows on a shroud.'

There fell a fearful silence on the place,
　While the scared guests saw Haroun from his throne
　Frown at the bard, and then, with a deep groan,
Hide in his trembling hands his weeping face.

Straightway a supple courtier standing by
　Cried to the singer, 'Blasted be the throat
　Which frights our master with a boding note
In lieu of mirthful music ; look to die.'

' Nay,' Haroun whispered, ' do not blame the bard ;

   He saw our soul benighted, and, like wind,

   Dispersed the veil of error.   Let him find

My richest gems too poor for his reward.'

GHAZEL.

IF the gracious girl I worship would but take my heart
  in hand,
I would give her for her beauty Ispahan and Samarcand.

But this lass, the very fairest trouble of our tranquil
  town,
Plucks all patience from my bosom, lifts my hopes to
  laugh them down.

She has slandered me, so be it; I forgive her, speaking
sooth,

For the harshest words fall softly from the scarlet lips
of youth;

Yet I dare not call her cruel, though she does me
grievous wrong,

For what lovely face is flattered by the proudest poet's
song?

Fill, then, friend, while wine remaineth, for in Paradise,
dear lad,

We shall sigh for Mosellay and weep the waves of Rocknabad.

Speak of wine and song and women ; cease, I pray, to
    seek in vain,
What that mystery most mystic called to-morrow may
    contain.

String thy pearls and sing them, Hafiz, for from
    heaven's golden bars
God has shed upon thy verses all the sweetness of the
    stars.

THE GRAVE OF OMAR-I-KHAYYAM.

I, NAMED Nizami, child of Samarcand,

The holy place whose towers aspire to heaven,

Whose domes are blue as heaven's inverted cup,

The consecrated shrine, head of Islam,

Whose heart is at Meccah, the happy spot

Where bloom the gardens of the Heart's Delight,

Where in the house upon the Shepherd's Hill

Wise men pursue the pathway of the stars—

I, even Nizami, write this record down

In God's name, merciful, compassionate,

A proof of his compassion.

When my youth

Burned in my body like a new-fed flame,

When wisdom seemed an easy flower to pluck,

And knowledge fruit that ripens in a day;

Ah me! that merry When so long ago

I was a pupil of that man of men,

Omar, the tent-maker of Naishapur,

That is Khorassan's crown, Omar the wise,

Whose wisdom read the golden laws of life,

And made them ours for ever in his songs,

Omar the star-gazer.

One day by chance,

I taxing all my student's store of wit

With thought of is and is not, good and bad,

And fondly dreaming that my fingers soon

Would close upon the key of heaven and earth,

I met my master in a garden walk,

Musing as was his wont, I knew not what,

Perhaps some better mode of marshalling

Those daily soldiers of the conquering years,

Perchance some subtler science which the stars

Ciphered in fire upon the vaulted sky

For him alone, perchance on some rare rhymes

Pregnant with mighty thoughts, or on some girl,

Star-eyed and cypress-slender, tulip-cheeked

And jasmine-bosomed, for he loved such well,

And deemed it wisdom.

                 Omar saw me not,

And would have passed me curtained in his

    thoughts ;

But I, perked up with youthful consequence

At mine own wisdom, plucked him by the sleeve,

And with grave salutation, as befits

The pupil to the master, stayed his course

And craved his patience.

　　　　　　　　　Omar gazed at me

With the grave sweetness which his servants loved,

And gave me leave to speak, which I, on fire

To tell the thing I thought, made haste to do,

And poured my babble in the master's ear

Of solving human doubt.

　　　　　　　　　When I had done,

And, panting, looked into my master's eyes

To read therein approval of my plan,

He turned his head, and for a little while

Waited in silence, while my petulant mind
Galloped again the course of argument
And found no flaw, all perfect.

                  Still he stood
Silent, and I, the riddle-reader, vexed
At long-delayed approval, touched again
His sleeve, and with impatient reverence
Said,

     'Master, speak, that I may garner up
In scented manuscripts the thoughts of price
That fall from Omar's lips.'

               He smiled again
In sweet forgiveness of my turbulent mood,
And with a kindly laughter in his eyes
He said,

'I have been thinking, when I die,

That I should like to slumber where the wind

May heap my tomb with roses.'

                           So he spoke,

And then with thoughtful face and quiet tread

He past and left me staring, most amazed

At such a pearl from such a sea of thought,

And marvelling that great philosophers

Can pay so little sometimes heed to truth

When truth is thrust before them.   God be praised !

I am wiser now, and grasp no golden key.

Years came and went, and Omar passed away,

First from those garden walks of Samarcand

Where he and I so often watched the moon

Silver the bosoms of the cypresses,

And so from out the circle of my life,

And in due season out of life itself;

And his great name became a memory

That clung about me like the scent of flowers

Beloved in boyhood, and the wheeling years

Ground pleasure into dust beneath my feet;

And so the world wagged till there came a day

When I that had been young and was not young,

I found myself in Naishapur, and there

Bethought me of my master dead and gone,

And the musk-scented preface of my youth.

Then to myself I said, 'Nizami, rise

And seek the tomb of Omar.'

                    So I sought,

And after seeking found, and, lo! it lay

Beyond a garden full of roses, full

As the third heaven is full of happy eyes;

And every wind that whispered through the trees

Scattered a heap of roses on his grave;

Yea, roses leaned, and from their odorous hearts

Rained petals on his marble monument,

Crimson as lips of angels.

                    Then my mind,

Sweeping the desert of departed years,

Leaped to that garden speech in Samarcand,

The cypress grove, my fretful questioning,

And the mild beauty of my master's face.

Then I knelt down and glorified Allah,

Who is compassionate and merciful,

That of his boundless mercy he forgave

This singing sinner ; for I surely knew

That all the leaves of every rose that dripped

Its tribute on the tomb where Omar sleeps,

Were tears and kisses that should smooth away

His record of offence ; for Omar sinned,

Since Omar was a man.

He wished to sleep

Beneath a veil of roses ; Heaven heard,

Forgave, and granted, and the perfumed pall

Hides the shrine's whiteness.   Glory to Allah !

OMAR ANSWERS.

Now by the memory of Kai Khosru,
Of Kaikobad, of Zal and Rustem too,
  O English singer rousing me from sleep,
The student of the stars will answer you.

For what avails it cycles to have lain
Since first the roses gushed their scented rain
  Upon my grave in Naishapur if men
In the world's winter take my name in vain ?

Through piled-up earth and ages echoes reach
My tranquil slumbers of an alien speech,
Blown over seas wherein strange doctors preach
Strange sermons on the things I thought to teach.

For, misinterpreting the songs I sung,   .
By vain desire and vain ambition stung,
   O for one hour of that lost age ! they cry,
That golden age when old Khayyam was young.

Fools who believe the world was otherwise
Than what it now is in the Persian's eyes,
   Or think the secret of content was found
Beneath the canopy of Persian skies.

Man is to-day what man was yesterday—
Will be to-morrow ; let him curse or pray,
  Drink or be dull, he learns not nor shall learn
The lesson that will laugh the world away.

The world as grey or just as golden shows,
The wine as sweet or just as bitter flows,
  For you as me ; and you, like me, may find
Perfume or canker in the reddest rose.

The tale of life is hard to understand ;
But while the cup waits ready to your hand,
  Drink and declare the summer roses blow
As red in London as in Samarcand.

Lips are as sweet to kiss and eyes as bright
As ever fluttered Omar with delight ;
  English or Persian, while the mouth is fair,
What can it matter how it says good-night ?

Whether the legend in the Book of Youth
Runs left or right, it reads a prayer for ruth ;
  The music of the bird upon the bough
Meant, and still means, no more nor less than truth.

The wisdom of the wisest of the wise
Is but the pinch of powder in the eyes
  Thrown by the fingers of the fiend, that we
True things from false may fail to recognise.

And not a pang which vexes human flesh,

And not a problem which the Sufis thresh,

   But scared my body or perplexed my soul,

And what I felt each man must feel afresh.

So, brother, by Allah! forbear to weep:

Life is a wine which you may drink as deep

   As ever I did, for the hour will come

When you, like old Khayyam, will fall asleep.

Therefore, O northern singer! prithee cease

To vex my sprite with questions. Know, thy lease

   Was by the selfsame Master made as mine;

Be patient, then, and let me sleep in peace.

PRINTED BY

SPOTTISWOODE AND CO., NEW-STREET SQUARE

LONDON

CPSIA information can be obtained at www.ICGtesting.com

231162LV00003B/177/P